Sports Innovations

INNOVATIONS IN BASEBALL

by Douglas Hustad

SportsZone

An Imprint of Abdo Publishing
abdobooks.com

abdobooks.com

Published by Abdo Publishing, a division of ABDO, PO Box 398166, Minneapolis, Minnesota 55439. Copyright © 2022 by Abdo Consulting Group, Inc. International copyrights reserved in all countries. No part of this book may be reproduced in any form without written permission from the publisher. SportsZone™ is a trademark and logo of Abdo Publishing.

Printed in the United States of America, North Mankato, Minnesota.
102021
012022

Cover Photos: Peter Joneleit/Cal Sport Media/Zuma Wire/AP Images, left; AP Images, right
Interior Photos: Goodwin & Co./Library of Congress, 5; Ben Margot/AP Images, 7, 23, 43; Joseph Sohm/Shutterstock Images, 8–9, 32; Michael Doolittle/Alamy, 11; Arturo Holmes/Shutterstock Images, 13; Jamie Lamor Thompson/Shutterstock Images, 17; Charles Knoblock/AP Images, 18; Tom Olmscheid/AP Images, 20–21; Shutterstock Images, 25; Mark Rucker/Transcendental Graphics/Getty Images Sports/Getty Images, 26–27; David J. Phillip/AP Images, 28; Eric Broder Van Dyke/Shutterstock Images, 31; Kent Weakley/Shutterstock Images, 35; AP Images, 37; Cliff Welch/Icon Sportswire/AP Images, 39; Doug Pensinger/Getty Images Sport/Getty Images, 41

Editor: Katie Chanez
Series Designer: Joshua Olson

Library of Congress Control Number: 2020949102

Publisher's Cataloging-in-Publication Data

Names: Hustad, Douglas, author.
Title: Innovations in baseball / by Douglas Hustad
Description: Minneapolis, Minnesota : Abdo Publishing, 2022 | Series: Sports innovations | Includes online resources and index.
Identifiers: ISBN 9781532195020 (lib. bdg.) | ISBN 9781098215330 (ebook)
Subjects: LCSH: Baseball--Juvenile literature. | Technological innovations--Juvenile literature. | Sports sciences--Juvenile literature. | Performance technology--Juvenile literature. | Baseball--Equipment and supplies--Juvenile literature. | Sports--Juvenile literature.
Classification: DDC 688.76--dc23

TABLE OF CONTENTS

CHAPTER 1

TOOLS OF
THE TRADE

Imagine stepping onto a baseball field in the 1860s. The uniforms and equipment would look quite different. Some of the rules would be different too. But some things haven't changed. The sport has always required a ball and a bat.

Back in the 1860s, players tried many different styles of bats. Many of them were homemade. Some had flat faces. Some were round. The only thing they all had in common was they were wood. But even the type of wood varied.

By 1870 the baseball rulebook had established guidelines for the bat. It had to be round. It had to be made of wood. And it could be no longer than 42 inches (107 cm) and no more than 2.5 inches (6.4 cm) wide. In modern Major League Baseball (MLB), that rule is basically the same.

Pete Browning helped pioneer the Louisville Slugger baseball bat.

CO. NY

The modern era of bat-making began in 1884. A 17-year-old woodworker named Bud Hillerich attended a game with his hometown's major league team, the Louisville Eclipse. Eclipse slugger Pete Browning broke his bat during the game, and Hillerich offered to make him a new one. Browning got three hits with his new bat the next day. The Louisville Slugger company was born. Louisville Slugger has been making baseball bats ever since. Eighty percent of the players in the National Baseball Hall of Fame used a Louisville Slugger bat.

THE WOOD MAKES IT GOOD

Because the rulebook only specified that a bat be made of wood, players were free to experiment with different kinds of wood. Ash was the most common choice for decades. In the late 1990s, maple bats started gaining popularity. Joe Carter of the Toronto Blue Jays was the first player to use a maple bat in a game in 1997.

San Francisco Giants slugger Barry Bonds was the most famous user of maple bats. Bonds started using them in 1999. In 2001 he set an MLB single-season record with 73 home runs. He went on to break the all-time career home run record as well. However, he was accused of getting some help by using illegal performance-enhancing drugs.

Toronto Blue Jays outfielder Joe Carter was the first MLB player to use a maple bat.

Over time, hitters discovered that maple bats shattered easily. And studies showed they didn't make the ball fly any farther than ash bats. But players loved how they felt on impact, so they kept using them. Just like the hitters who played more than a century before, today's sluggers continue to experiment in the search for the perfect bat.

A METALLIC BOOST

Wooden bats have always been the standard for MLB. But at lower levels of baseball, wood was not always ideal. Wood bats break, forcing young players to buy new ones often. And they require more skill to hit the ball far, which could frustrate young players.

Children's leagues began using aluminum bats because they are lighter and more durable than wood bats.

In the 1970s, manufacturers were working hard to find a solution that didn't involve wood. The Easton company made an aluminum bat. Louisville Slugger quickly followed. The results were mostly positive. The bats didn't break easily, so they lasted a long time. And they performed similarly to wood bats. Soon, players from Little League to college were using aluminum bats.

But aluminum had some drawbacks. Older players could generate a lot of power with their swings. Balls flew off aluminum bats at deadly speeds, putting pitchers and infielders in danger. And college scores were starting to resemble those of football games. In the 1998 College World Series championship game, the University of Southern California (USC) defeated Arizona State 21–14. Something had to be done to make the game safer and lower-scoring.

In 1999 the National Collegiate Athletic Association (NCAA) implemented a new rule stating that the "drop" between length and weight could be no greater than three—that is, a 34-inch (86 cm) bat could weigh no less than 31 ounces (0.88 kg). This helped a bit, but a new standard in 2011 was even more effective. It governed how quickly a ball flies off a bat. The change made the bats perform much more like wood.

LEATHER AND YARN

Just as hitters used to make their own bats, pitchers used to make their own baseballs. These resembled modern baseballs; they consisted of a core that was wrapped in yarn and leather. But there was no single method of producing them.

A baseball's core is made of cork covered in rubber. It's wrapped in yarn, and a leather covering is added.

This resulted in some balls that flew really far and some that were "dead."

The Harwood & Sons company began producing balls with the modern "figure eight" design in 1858. The name comes from the two leather panels shaped like the number eight that make up the ball's cover. But the weight and consistency of balls continued to vary.

A. G. Spalding was a pitcher for the Boston Red Sox. He made his own balls and was one of the game's most successful hurlers. In 1876 he shared his baseball design with the National League (NL), which was in its first season. Not only did Spalding's ball become the standard, he founded his own sporting goods company. The Spalding company made the official NL ball for the next century.

ALL YOU NEED IS GLOVE

Spalding had a hand in the invention of the baseball glove, too. His teammate Charles C. Waite first wore a glove during a game in 1875. Waite was mocked for it, as playing barehanded was the style in those days. But Spalding thought using a glove was a good idea. His company began making gloves, and Spalding started wearing one in 1877.

Early gloves did not look much like the gloves of today. They were more like work gloves but without fingers. They did not help catch the ball. They only provided limited hand protection.

Players gradually came around to the idea of using a glove. By 1900 every MLB player was using one. Gloves began to come with more padding. In 1920 St. Louis Cardinals pitcher Bill Doak created the first glove with webbing between the fingers. He sold it to the Rawlings company, which pioneered the modern glove design and still makes them today.

BEHIND THE PLATE

No position has more specialized equipment than catcher.

Surprisingly, catchers wore no safety protection in the early

Early catchers wore no safety equipment, but modern ones have more gear than any other player.

days of baseball. They stood much farther back from the plate in those days, but injuries were still very common.

The catcher's mask was one of the first pieces of protective equipment in any sport. James Tyng was the first baseball player known to have worn one. Tyng played for Harvard University in 1878, and team manager Frederick Thayer was the man who designed the mask. When Tyng took the field, fans made fun of him for being afraid of the ball. But Tyng had the last laugh. His mask now resides in the National Baseball Hall of Fame.

Other elements of the modern catching equipment developed throughout the rest of the 1800s. Early catcher's gloves were basically thick pieces of leather that were worn to stop the ball. Catcher Gus Niarhos came up with the idea to have a "hinge" in the glove to trap the ball. He cut a slit in his glove in the 1950s, which led to the modern catcher's mitt design.

THE PITCHER HELMET

Despite standing just 60 feet 6 inches (18.4 m) from bat-wielding sluggers, pitchers wear no safety equipment. In 2014 MLB approved a design for the first pitcher helmet. San Diego Padres relief pitcher Alex Torres became the first player to wear one in a game that season. But the idea failed to catch on with other pitchers.

THE HELMET

In 1920 Cleveland Indians shortstop Ray Chapman was killed after being hit in the head with a pitch. Despite this shocking event, batting helmets still failed to catch on in MLB for another 50 years. Some players experimented with plastic inserts inside their caps. But modern helmets were still a long way off. MLB didn't mandate them for all new players until 1971.

Bob Montgomery was the last player to not wear a batting helmet. He retired in 1979. The modern helmet with an earflap would not be required until 1983. And that was only for new players. Gary Gaetti retired in 2000 as the last hitter who wore a helmet without an earflap.

Safety is just one area of innovation in baseball over its long history. Other innovations have improved performance and made the game more exciting. Even through all these changes, baseball has remained the same basic game that fans know and love.

CHAPTER 2

MAJOR RULE
CHANGES

Players used to have to swing at a ball for it to be called a strike. That is how the term "strike" was named. Until the 1850s, a player could take as many pitches as he wanted without swinging. If he struck at the ball three times without getting a hit, only then was he out.

The National Association of Base Ball Players was the first organization in charge of baseball in the United States. Its 1858 rulebook contains the first attempt at establishing a strike zone. It allowed umpires to call a penalty strike if the batter repeatedly failed to swing at "good" balls.

But there were no real rules on what counted as a good pitch. The concept of a strike zone didn't appear in a rulebook until 1887. The strike zone was defined as the width of the plate from the batter's knees to his shoulders. Today's strike

caption:

Despite the rise of instant replay in many sports, balls and strikes are still determined entirely by umpires. Coaches and managers cannot dispute those calls.

zone is a little smaller. But it is still up to the interpretation of each umpire.

BRING DOWN THE MOUND

That larger strike zone was still the standard in the 1960s. Pitchers became dominant that decade. They threw faster than ever and had a big advantage over hitters.

Before the 1969 season, pitching mounds were considerably higher than they are today.

The pitcher's mound was higher in those days. It was 15 inches (38 cm) tall, but some teams built theirs even higher. The rule was not strictly enforced.

That all changed after 1968. Called "The Year of the Pitcher," pitchers ruled the game more than ever before. The collective batting average for the league was .237, by far the lowest in history. One in five games resulted in a shutout. The MLB-wide earned-run average (ERA) was 2.98, the first time it had dipped below 3.00 since the demise of the so-called "dead-ball era" (before 1920).

To restore balance to the game, MLB lowered the mound to 10 inches (25 cm) in 1969. That year, the league batting average climbed to .248 and the ERA rose to 3.61 as teams increased their scoring by more than a run per game on average.

THE DESIGNATED HITTER

Since the beginning of baseball, all nine players who took the field also took their turn at the plate. But also since the beginning, most pitchers proved to be poor hitters.

They spent more time working on their pitching than their hitting, so as a result, the pitcher's spot in the lineup was usually counted as an easy out.

The idea of a designated hitter (DH) to hit in place of the pitcher arose as early as the 1890s. William Chase Temple, the owner of the Pittsburgh Pirates, brought it up in 1891.

Using a designated hitter allows aging sluggers such as Nelson Cruz to extend their careers.

The rule was actually voted on by the NL in 1892 but was defeated.

In the years to come, some prominent voices continued to argue for the DH. Philadelphia Athletics owner and manager

Connie Mack was one of the biggest supporters in the early 1900s. It was another Athletics owner, Charlie Finley, who revived the issue in the 1970s, shortly after the team had moved to Oakland, California.

Finley saw the designated hitter as a way to attract more fans. It would boost offense and add more excitement to the game. Finley convinced the other American League (AL) owners of this, and on January 11, 1973, the league voted to adopt the DH.

The American League and National League (NL) are considered separate leagues governed by MLB. Most rules apply to both leagues. But in 1973, NL owners voted against adopting the DH. Through the 2019 season the National League continued to resist, though NL teams used the DH in interleague and postseason games played in AL parks. The 2020 season was shortened due to the COVID-19 pandemic, prompting MLB to temporarily require the National League to use the DH.

Many baseball fans had grown to love the addition of the designated hitter. The position produced some great hitters who wound up having Hall of Fame careers. It also gave aging fan favorites a chance to stay in the game. But it also took away some strategy. Managers did not have to worry about

David Ortiz was the World Series Most Valuable Player in 2013 as a DH.

pinch-hitting for the pitcher if his turn in the order came around when an out might kill a rally. Baseball fans still enjoy arguing both for and against the DH in the National League. Many are passionate about whether or not to use it across MLB.

CHAPTER 3

MAKING
MODERN MLB

The National League was founded in 1876. Throughout the late 1800s, a few other leagues emerged to challenge it. In 1884 the NL-champion Providence Grays agreed to meet the New York Metropolitans of the American Association to determine a champion of baseball. This was the first playoff series known as the World Series.

But the American Association folded not long after. No league managed to survive alongside the NL until 1901. That was when the American League began play.

For two years, AL teams tried their best to convince top NL players to turn their backs on their old teams and join the new league. After two years of fighting, the two leagues came to an agreement in 1903. Each league would honor the contracts of the other league. And they created the modern World Series.

caption: Starting in 1967, the winner of the World Series was given a trophy. In 1985 it was named the Commissioner's Trophy.

Boston's Huntington Avenue Grounds was home to the opening game of the first World Series in 1903.

Before the World Series, there were no playoffs. The team with the best regular-season record was deemed the champion. Fans were thrilled to see how the top teams from the two best baseball leagues matched up. With only a few exceptions, the World Series has been played every season since 1903.

EXPANDING THE PLAYOFFS

The path to the World Series has changed over the years. Before 1969 the team with the best record in each

league qualified. But starting that season, MLB expanded
its playoff race. It broke each league into two divisions. The
division winners played each other in a league championship
series for the right to go to the World Series.

Bud Selig became commissioner of baseball in 1992. He
oversaw changes to baseball that upset some of the game's
longtime fans. For example, each league added a third division
in 1994. To make an even playoff field, it also added a fourth
playoff team, the wild card. This was the team with the best
record that did not win its division. This opened a path to the

The addition of wild cards in the playoffs gives teams like the 2019 Nationals, who finished second in a strong division, a shot at winning the World Series.

World Series that didn't exist before. And in 2012, MLB added a second wild-card team from each league. The two wild cards faced off in a wild-card round.

Many traditionalists felt it was wrong to award a playoff spot to a team that failed to win its division. But the wild-card spot also kept more teams, such as the 2019 Washington Nationals, in the playoff race longer. The Nationals got off to a bad start to the season. They were 19–31 on May 24. But they rebounded and qualified for the playoffs thanks to the wild card. They then went on to win the World Series. They were the seventh wild-card team to win it all.

INTERLEAGUE PLAY

Another Selig innovation was interleague play. Until 1997 the only times AL and NL teams faced each other was during the preseason, the All-Star Game, and the World Series. But interleague play became a feature of every team's schedule starting in 1997.

This was another move that upset baseball purists. But many other fans were excited. They got to watch players who normally never came to their team's ballpark.

Interleague play was limited to a couple of series per team at first. But in 2013, MLB shifted the Houston Astros from the NL to the AL. That gave each league 15 teams, or three five-team divisions. It was great for parity between the leagues. However, in order for every team to be playing on a given day, at least one game had to feature an AL team versus an NL team. Interleague play was no longer a novelty. It was just part of the modern game of baseball.

CHAPTER 4

OLD BECOMES NEW AT
THE BALLPARK

Baseball expanded into many new markets starting in 1961. Some fans grumbled that baseball was breaking with tradition. Those changes were even more evident on the fields of play themselves.

Fans who grew up watching games at Wrigley Field in Chicago and Ebbets Field in New York cherished memories of those palaces of baseball. Fans sat close to the action, even in the upper deck. They were designed with only baseball in mind.

Many teams in the 1960s and 1970s moved into multipurpose stadiums. They shared them with National Football League (NFL) teams. Teams had shared stadiums before. For instance, the Chicago Bears once shared Wrigley

caption: Fenway Park, home of the Boston Red Sox, is the oldest ballpark in MLB. It was built in 1912.

FENWAY PARK
1903
1904
1912
1915
1916
1918
1946
1967
1975
1986
2004
2007
WM
Ninety Nine

The construction of Oriole Park at Camden Yards in Baltimore touched off a new wave of retro ballpark design.

Field with the Chicago Cubs, and the Detroit Lions played at Briggs Stadium, home of the AL's Detroit Tigers.

But those were baseball parks that squeezed football fields within their walls. The first stadium built specifically to house both baseball and football was Robert F. Kennedy Memorial Stadium in Washington, DC. It opened in 1961. Its design was circular, providing ample room for either a baseball field or a football field. Numerous other stadiums with this design concept opened over the next 20 years. They all utilized the same basic design, which is why annoyed fans referred to them as "cookie-cutter" stadiums.

These stadiums saved money for cities that could build just one stadium instead of two. They also used artificial turf to save on grass maintenance. But the fan experience was not ideal for baseball. Many of the seats were far away from the field. And the seats faced straight ahead toward the middle of the field, which was ideal for football. In a true baseball park, the seats face home plate.

BACK TO THE CLASSICS

The Baltimore Orioles played in a multipurpose stadium until 1992. That was when they opened Oriole Park at Camden Yards. The ballpark was created only for baseball. It had all the conveniences of a modern stadium but was designed to look like the classic ballparks. Its green seats and brick walls reminded fans of Wrigley Field. A high fence in right field was similar to Fenway Park's Green Monster. Camden Yards immediately became the talk of the league.

It was so popular that many teams wanted one just like it. The Texas Rangers, Colorado Rockies, and Cleveland Indians all built similar parks within three years. Many more opened in the years that followed.

Another feature of cookie-cutter stadiums was they were often located far from the center of the city their teams represented. Camden Yards opened right in the heart of Baltimore. It incorporated an old warehouse into a right field plaza. San Diego's Petco Park used the corner of an old warehouse as its left field foul pole when it opened in 2004. These features helped connect the ballparks to the city's neighborhoods.

DAY OR NIGHT, RAIN OR SHINE

Baseball was played during the day until 1935. Then Cincinnati Reds general manager Larry MacPhail saw a way to make his team stand out. He introduced MLB to night baseball when his team played the Philadelphia Phillies under the lights on May 24, 1935. Fans loved being able to work a day job and still see a game at night. And fears of players having trouble seeing the ball proved to be unfounded. Night baseball took off, and day games—especially on weekdays—soon became rarer.

There was one notable holdout. The last team to install lights was the Chicago Cubs, who didn't play a night game at Wrigley Field until 1988. Even today, the Cubs play the fewest night games in MLB. It is part of an agreement to not disrupt the residential neighborhood surrounding Wrigley Field.

Weather remained an issue, however. Rain and cold conditions make it difficult to play baseball. And hot, humid

MLB teams play an average of 54 home night games during the regular season. The Chicago Cubs can only play 43 due to city rules.

weather is hard on fans. The Houston Astrodome, which opened in 1965, was MLB's first indoor stadium. The first park that had a roof that could open and close was Montreal's Olympic Stadium. But the roof rarely worked properly and eventually was permanently closed.

Toronto's SkyDome opened in 1989. It featured the first fully functioning retractable roof. Toronto's cold climate in the spring and fall made a roof necessary. But it also allowed fans to enjoy the summer. By the 2020 season, six more parks were built with retractable roofs.

ASTROTURF

Indoor baseball was a huge innovation when Houston's Astrodome opened in 1965. The Astros tried to grow grass with skylights, but the grass died. It led to the creation of the first artificial turf for indoor use, which was fittingly called Astroturf.

CHAPTER 5

OUTTHINKING THE OPPONENT

Over the years, flame-throwing closers such as Bruce Sutter, Dennis Eckersley, and Aroldis Chapman have been some of the game's biggest stars. But back in the 1860s, baseball teams didn't have relief pitchers. Unless the starting pitcher got hurt, he could not come out of the game. If he was having a bad day on the mound, he could only switch places with another fielder.

Even when that rule changed in 1889, most starters still pitched the whole game. At the beginning of the 1903 season, Giants manager John McGraw proposed using a second pitcher when his starter got tired. But McGraw feared being mocked if his second pitcher lost the game. He gave up on the plan.

Firpo Marberry of the Washington Senators became the first prominent full-time reliever in the 1920s. Manager Bucky Harris

caption: **New York Yankee Joe Page was one of the first relievers to save 20 games in a single season.**

often used Marberry for three innings at a time. He finished fourth on the team in innings pitched in 1924, with 35 of his 50 appearances coming in relief.

With the New York Yankees, Harris was the manager for another prominent reliever in the 1940s. In 1949 Joe Page became the first pitcher to save 20 games in a season since Marberry did it in 1925. Only nobody knew what a save was yet.

THE CLOSER

The save is a statistic that was devised in 1960 by Chicago sportswriter Jerome Holtzman. It was the first stat specifically tracked to evaluate relief pitchers. It became an official MLB statistic in 1969. That was around the time that managers saw the value of using one strong pitcher to finish off close games.

Strong relief pitchers became known as firemen, because they came in to shut down the opponent in the game's most dangerous spots. Many firemen pitched more than one inning at a time. But in 1989, Oakland Athletics' manager Tony La Russa noticed that his closer, Dennis Eckersley, seemed to perform better the less he pitched.

La Russa started using Eckersley to pitch just one inning at a time. He came on in the ninth to lock down an A's win. Use of

Oakland's Dennis Eckersley became one of MLB's first closers to specialize in throwing just one inning per game.

a "closer" pitcher in this role took off. All teams sought elite relievers to close games.

Yankees pitcher Mariano Rivera started his career just as one-inning closers became popular in the 1990s. He became the league's all-time saves leader, compiling 652 of them in 19 seasons. In 2019 he became the first unanimous selection to the Baseball Hall of Fame.

SHIFT IN THINKING

In 1946 Boston Red Sox slugger Ted Williams was tormenting the American League. Trying to slow down the future Hall of Famer, Cleveland Indians manager Lou Boudreau stacked his fielders on the right side of the diamond. That was where Williams got most of his hits. But the shift didn't help— Williams hit three home runs that day.

Boudreau was not the first manager to try a defensive shift. But the shift became associated with trying to contain hitters who often pulled the ball. A left-handed pull hitter hits most balls between first and second base, while a right-handed pull hitter usually drives balls between second and third.

In 2006 another Red Sox slugger tormented the league. David Ortiz frequently got the best of the Tampa Bay Rays.

The Tampa Bay Rays put three infielders on the right side of second base—including one in short right field—to defend a left-handed pull hitter.

Rays manager Joe Maddon noticed in Ortiz's stats that he mostly hit to right field.

Maddon placed his shortstop and second baseman in short right field. The left fielder and centerfielder moved closer to the right fielder. The third baseman moved into left field. He was the lone player on the left side of the field.

It was called the "Ortiz Shift." Other teams tried similar shifts against Ortiz. After hitting over .300 in 2004 and 2005, Ortiz hit under .300 in 2006. As more teams started analyzing statistics, the shift became popular league-wide in the 2010s.

CRUNCHING THE NUMBERS

The study of statistics is known as analytics. In baseball, it is known as sabermetrics. Baseball writer Bill James was a member of the Society for American Baseball Research (SABR) in the 1970s and '80s. He came up with the term sabermetrics while applying advanced statistical analysis to the game of baseball.

Statistics have been a big part of baseball for a long time. The box score was invented in 1859. These small bits of information allowed fans to know what happened in a game and how each player had performed.

Sabermetrics was designed to both summarize how a player or team performed and also predict how they might do in the future. One of the statistics James invented is runs created. This measures how a player contributes to the runs his team scores. Statistics like these can reveal more about a player's abilities than a simple batting average or home run total.

James's research spread to the major leagues. Oakland A's general manager Billy Beane was a fan of James's work and used it in the early 2000s. By valuing different stats than what other teams were looking for, Beane was able to acquire the players he wanted for less money. Despite spending

Oakland manager Billy Beane, *left*, used sabermetrics to build his team instead of relying on traditional methods.

less on players than most teams, Beane's A's were a regular playoff contender.

However, not everyone embraced analytics. Many owners, managers, and even fans preferred using traditional stats and their eyes to evaluate players. But teams did not want to get left behind. Every team in MLB established some kind of analytics department. Teams gathered more information than ever on players.

Sabermetrics is just one example of how people look at baseball differently today than in the 1800s. People play the game differently, too. Still, fans love the game all the same.

TIMELINE

1878
James Tyng becomes the first catcher known to wear a mask in a game for Harvard University.

1884
Bud Hillerich creates the first Louisville Slugger bat for slugger Pete Browning. Browning gets three hits the next day, and today, most MLB players use a Louisville Slugger model bat.

1903
The AL and NL come to an agreement that includes setting up a playoff series pitting the league champions against each other, later called the World Series.

1920
Cleveland Indians shortstop Ray Chapman is killed after being hit in the head by a pitch, but it would be decades before all players would be required to wear batting helmets.

1935
The Cincinnati Reds become the first MLB team to host a night game when they play the Philadelphia Phillies on May 24.

1969
After a historically dominant season by pitchers, MLB lowers the height of the pitcher's mound to give some advantage back to the hitters.

1969
The save becomes an official MLB statistic, leading to the development of the closer, a one-inning specialist pitcher whose job is to pitch the last inning of a win.

1973
The AL adopts a rule that each team may use a DH in its lineup to bat for the pitcher. The NL chooses not to adopt the DH.

1992
The Baltimore Orioles open Camden Yards, the first in a series of ballparks designed to remind fans of classic ballparks of the early 1900s.

2013
The Houston Astros switch from the NL to the AL, requiring teams to schedule interleague games throughout the season.

BREAKING THE COLOR LINE

Until 1947, there was an informal agreement among MLB owners not to allow any Black players in the league. Brooklyn Dodgers owner Branch Rickey assigned his scouts to watch on the Negro Leagues, the only professional league for Black people. Rickey knew immense talent was being kept out of MLB. He discovered Jackie Robinson, who became the first Black player in MLB on April 15, 1947. Robinson played 10 years in MLB and made the Hall of Fame.

FREE AGENCY

Until 1976 MLB players did not have much say in what team they played for. Baseball had a reserve clause that gave a team the right to retain players unless it released or traded them. The first player to challenge this system was St. Louis Cardinals outfielder Curt Flood in 1969. Flood wanted the right to reject a trade to the Phillies and become a free agent. Flood sued baseball in 1970. Flood lost, and he never played in the majors again. But he started the process that dismantled the reserve clause and established free agency in MLB in 1976.

CURVEBALL

Candy Cummings is believed to have invented the curveball in the 1870s. He was throwing shells as a teenager and noticed they curved in the air. He tried doing it with a baseball and perfected the pitch by college. For a long time, fans believed the pitch didn't actually curve, but rather was just an illusion.

batting average
A player's number of hits divided by the number of at-bats.

commissioner
The chief executive of a sports league.

contender
A person or team that has a good chance at winning a championship.

folded
Went out of business.

manager
The head coach of a baseball team.

markets
Geographic areas with a pro sports team.

mitt
A type of glove that does not have individual fingers.

novelty
Something known for its new, unusual nature.

slugger
A player best known for hitting home runs.

statistics
A collection of numbers or data.

webbing
The interlocked sections of leather in the fingers of a baseball glove.

MORE INFORMATION

BOOKS

Gitlin, Marty. *Great Baseball Debates*. Minneapolis, MN: Abdo Publishing, 2019.

Kortemeier, Todd. *Total Baseball*. Minneapolis, MN: Abdo Publishing, 2017.

Williams, Doug. *Baseball Record Breakers*. Minneapolis, MN: Abdo Publishing, 2016.

ONLINE RESOURCES

Booklinks
NONFICTION NETWORK
FREE! ONLINE NONFICTION RESOURCES

To learn more about innovations in baseball, please visit **abdobooklinks.com** or scan this QR code. These links are routinely monitored and updated to provide the most current information available.

ABOUT THE AUTHOR

Douglas Hustad is a freelance author primarily of science and history books for young people. He, his wife, and their two dogs live in the northern suburbs of San Diego, California.